# I Remember

By

Michelle D. Griggs, M.S., M.S.

All the information contained in this book is based on the life experiences and opinions perceived and expressed by the author.

No part of this book may be reproduced or transmitted in any form or by any means electronically or mechanically, including photocopying or recording without prior written consent by the author or the publisher.

This book is printed in the United States.

Publisher:

Rose Gold Publishing, LLC

www.rosegoldpublishingllc.com

Copyright@2019 Michelle D. Griggs, MS., MS.

All rights reserved.

ISBN - 13: 978-1-733-2638-1-8
ISBN - 10: 1-7332638-1-0

# FOREWORD

By Lillie Pearl Bullock

To My Daughter Michelle Denise Charles Griggs on her first book, "I REMEMBER."

I want to take a moment to tell you about her.

Michelle was born on January 17, 1968, at Rockford Memorial Hospital in Rockford, IL. As a child, I saw the intelligent, ambitious, driven, and sincere kindness that bespeaks of the person she is today.

In 1971, we moved to Oakland, then to Salina California, where she attended grade school at Soberanus and later La Joya Schools. When she was ten years old, we moved back to Freeport, and she attended Taylor Park School, then Carl Sandburg Middle School. While in the 5th grade, a fellow student told her that she was "dumb" because she stumbled over words when she was reading. She didn't know it at the time that she was dyslexic. But Michelle took that as a direct challenge. And she began to read. ALL THE TIME. And "read" she did. Every book within her reach. Even today, she is a voracious reader.

Later, she attended Freeport Junior and Senior High school where she joined the cheerleading squad and sang in the Concert Choir. She furthered her education at Highland Community College then Illinois State University in Bloomington, Il. She received two master's degrees in Curriculum and Instruction with a focus in Multicultural Education and the second from the University of Missouri in Special Education with a K-12 Cross-Categorical degree.

I value my daughter Michelle's opinions and her sincere honesty in all of her endeavors. She works hard at all she attempts. She put her real feelings out in this book.

Congratulations, Michelle. Your father, sisters, and brothers; your entire family and I are proud of you.

Sincerely,

Lillie Pearl Hilton Charles Bullock (aka) Mom

# I Remember

By

Michelle D. Griggs, M.S., M.S.

## DEDICATION

This book is dedicated to my children August and Myles Griggs and Daniel Curry. They are the light of my life, the joy in my heart, and the laughter in my eyes. I love you all very much.

This is my remembering your father so that he is never forgotten.

# ACKNOWLEDGEMENTS

"Stop feeling guilty for living"

The phrase that helped me look into my healing process, which I never thought I needed in the first place, was said to me by my mother Lillie P. Bullock. My FIRST Shero and truest support system. She told me this, after my husband Charles had passed.

She told me that I had been given the gift of two children to raise and that it was my responsibility to be the best mother possible by letting go.

The next time I heard those words, it came from my dear friend and publisher, Mrs. Dolly Cortes. She and another dear friend, Luz-Marie Caro, not only encouraged me to not feel guilty for living, but also to look inside and remember the things I loved about being married to Charles. To remember all of the positive experiences that we shared. They also encouraged me to let go of my past and my anger after he passed away.

Yes, I had anger. And, it went in every direction.

A very special thanks go out to my Aunt Sandra Kay Hilton (God rest her beautiful soul). She helped me to see what it was that I liked about myself and encouraged me to seek out what I truly wanted. She encouraged me, at an early age to "write it down" and keep a journal. Thanks, Aunt San.

Dr. Norvella Carter, my college mentor, and a friend was the first to help me acknowledge that I was "an excellent writer"- her words…. I want to thank her for that and hope that all she taught me and encouraged me to do while in college is given here in these words.

All of these women are my personal Sheros. Each of them, in their own way, gave me a reason to think further and to dig deeper. They taught me to depend on God and look at myself to get the process started. In their own unique ways, each one encouraged me to trust the Lord's direction, trust my instincts and to do the right thing.

I am grateful for this encouragement and the love and support they have all shown me. I hope that you enjoy this work as much as I love sharing it with you.

I share these memories and the love of them with my friends and family. I share them with the world. I thank the Lord for the love He allowed me to share with Charles and, that it continues to live on through my three wonderful children.

Thank you and bless each of you today and every day.

# Introduction

***I Remember Charles***

I remember you.

You said you loved me. I remember, I believed you.

I believed in you. You said that you accepted me.

You listened to me. I remember I was glad of that.

That made you beautiful.

I remember happy times; I remember good and bad.

I remember you happy; I remember you sad

I remember you angry; I remember you lonely

I remember you missing your son.

I remember your smile. I loved that smile.

I remember you laughing.

I remember how much we loved laughing at any time.

I remember I loved you with all my heart in spite of the challenges that drew us apart.

I remember the day our sons were born, the pride you felt kept us all warm.

So much I remember, for so many days, there were so many changes in so many ways.

I remember, I remember your beautiful art; you had such great talent, a true expression of your heart.

You wrote so much, and with that, we lived well. Too bad, it all turned to hell.

I remember praying for you. I remember God answered me too.

Thank you for sharing your light with us all. We vow to remember you.

You were my best friend, my confident, and my lover. You were the truest excellent friend.

You held my heart in such a way that I know I will never find that one great thing, all else will pale, since we were left behind.

Thank you. Thank you for loving me and for letting me be part of you. Thank you for giving me my three children to love. Thank you for this experience, as pain filled as it has been.

Thank you so much, until we see you again.

Michelle D. Griggs,                                   April 2014

# TABLE OF MEMORIES

| | |
|---|---|
| I Remember Charles | 13 |
| I Remember, Can He Talk! | 15 |
| I Remember, Our Firsts… | 18 |
| I Remember, His Art Work | 26 |
| I Remember, His Love for Music | 34 |
| I Remember, Daniel | 37 |
| I Remember, August and Myles | 50 |
| I Remember, The Illness that Killed Him | 55 |
| My Family Remembers | 61 |
| I Remember, As Told by My Children | 64 |
| Picking Up the Pieces | 69 |

## I Remember Charles

I met my husband on a Thursday.

I remember rushing into my office and thinking, "Oh God! I have waaaay too much work to catch up on!" At the time, I was a full-time graduate student for the Department of Curriculum and Instruction at Illinois State University.

My office was located in the basement, of DeGarmo Hall and I had been passing by the study desks located there daily.

The day I met him; I had actually been sitting on a very nice, handwritten introduction note from that he had placed in my mailbox about two weeks earlier.

The note read,

*"Hello, my name is Charles, and I've watched you for a while. I've seen you in passing and thought what a nice young lady you must be. It encourages me to see you even though you're very active and busy. I hope that we can sit down and have a conversation. I'd like to get to know you. When you can, please give me a call if you're interested.*

*Thanks, Sincerely, Charles Griggs."*

I read the letter and smiled, I put it in my inbox intending to call when I got the chance.

When I called him back, again… 2 weeks later, I'd left him a short message thanking him for his note and said that if he had time and I was available, he should stop in and say hi if I was there.

Within 15 minutes, I noticed someone outside my door on the campus phone. I was about to close the door, but then I hear a semi-quiet knock, and there he was.

He was standing there in a black leather jacket and blue jeans looking a bit shy but smiling at me.

*"Hi, I'm Charles, I just got your message, and here I am… stopping by, as you said."*

He was not at all what I expected.

This tall well-mannered man with beautiful handwriting was smiling down at me and waiting for me to invite him into my office. He didn't seem like my type at all, and I felt kind of awkward at having him take me up on my message so quickly. I had hoped to have some time to process that I had responded to this guy! But here he was.

I did invite him to sit for what I thought would be a few minutes, and we ended up talking for about 45 minutes. He took me to lunch at the Chinese food restaurant near campus, and I can truly say that we had been together ever since.

## I Remember, Can He Talk!

Charles was definitely a talker.

I remember talking to him for hours on the phone each night the first week we met. I had NEVER had conversations where I had laughed so hard, nor thought so deeply with someone in my entire life. He was always such a smart deep thinker! I was intimidated a great deal at first. He made me feel so powerful but, so inadequate at the same time. I remember thinking, Lord …who is this man??!! All the time. My rush of emotions was very strong, and I had not wanted to lose that or bore him in any way. But we had a real conversation! It wasn't about a lot of sex or subjects that I was totally uninterested in. It was about life, love, and pain. It was about music and sports and all sorts of things. It was about the crazy things happening on the news, on his job or my job, or things with his family or with my family as well.

I remember our first conversation. Of course, it was the usual getting to know your stuff like, where are you from, what's your favorite color, what do you do in your spare time. We held a two-hour conversation together that afternoon and went to lunch and then we talked for another four hours on the phone that night! I kept thinking that we were going to run out of things to talk about. But we never did.

I was so excited to be able to speak so freely and so candidly, about everything from my disgust with the classes I had taken, to the ideas of current events and, even how sexy I thought Allen Payne (a yummy actor) was. I remember laughing so hard at a Star Trek episode with him just from how he would explain the thing! I will never forget his perspective on the episode entitled, "The Trouble with Tribbles."

I am still shaking my head and hearing his laughter.

He made me a little jealous when he described how much he just loooved Janet Jackson. (Can you see my eyes rolling back in my head?) We discussed who our heroes were, which, to our surprise, was the same person in our lives. This was our mothers. We hailed these warriors for their lives, their similarities, their strengths, their evident love for God, and for their love for us as their children. I know that we were both loved and cared for by our mothers.

I truly admire Mrs. Oralene Write. I know that Charles loved and admired Lillie Pearl (my mom). They had a great relationship, and I had an equally great relationship with his mother and father. One thing I prayed for was to have excellent in-laws. God truly answered that prayer. I have no doubt in my mind that my In-Laws Mr. and Mrs. Thomas Write, are currently residing in heaven.

As we continued to date, our conversation progressed in such a way that I gained a very clear insight into just how thoughtful Charles was.

He was polite, a bit soft spoken, kind-hearted, and never full of himself. He knew how to make me laugh! He was extremely intelligent and light-hearted most of the time. He was also a shy person who had a lot to say about a lot of things. I honestly didn't really pick up on the shyness until we were actually alone together on our second date. It was fun to get to know him and to see him open up. He also helped me to pen up more as well. There is nothing like a great thoughtful conversation to get to know someone. I remember... Smiling, I remember smiling A LOT.

## I Remember, Our Firsts…

The first Christmas I spent with Charles; we were still dating. He was a very quiet person and NEVER talked about his home life or his troubles. But I found out that he was staying in Bloomington because he couldn't make it home that year. It broke my heart to think that he would be there, in Bloomington, all by himself. When I called him after I had gotten home to Freeport and he told me this. By this time, it was almost Christmas Eve. I immediately felt hurt for him and angry that he had not mentioned it until *AFTER* I had gone home for the break. So about 30 minutes later, my eldest sister Estelle and I took off and went to pick him up. He was so happy to see us and so surprised that I actually drove the two and a half hours just for him. He actually had just gotten off work. We happened to catch him walking into his apartment.

I remember the happy expression on his face when he saw us. It was a SHEER surprise. I remember thinking about how much I enjoyed his smiling at me like he did. The ride back to Freeport was again, a great conversation.

Once we got in, he was able to rest, and we went out to do some shopping – He COULD NOT be in our house and not have a Christmas gift of some kind. We got him a sweater and some socks. He wore that sweater until he couldn't fit it and, I made him get rid of it.

I am smiling at that memory.

I remember other firsts too, our first kiss; interesting and sweet. He pecked me on my lips twice and then backed away. I just grinned, shook my head, and said goodnight. Every time after that was better. Trust me. (Smiling at remembering that).

I remember the first time we spent 24 hours together.... BEFORE we were married. See, we both shared very traditional "old fashioned" values so, we never slept together before marriage. Once we decided that we were going to get married, he made plans to get out of his apartment. I was ecstatic because he had the world worst roommate ever! (Can't even go there).

But in the meantime, he was going to be homeless for about six days. So, I suggest he just move in with me. He was so reluctant to live with me! I had two bedrooms apartment, so he took the extra one until we were married. I for one was very honored that he respected me enough to remain chaste, but I was also a bit anxious because I had never had anyone in the apartment that wasn't family, or a friend traveling in and out for a visit. It was an experience! He was so neat! Hahahaha! He was also very reluctant to really make himself at home. True enough it was "My Space," but he was welcome to every part of it.

Our first week of living together was defiantly an interesting experience. I truly got to know myself and him better. Once we were married, I had to get used to him actually sleeping in my bed, being in my space, sharing the bathroom all of the things you never think of when your single.

One of our first arguments we had as a married couple took place just 24 hours after our nuptials... We were married, in my townhouse apartment at the time, by my Pastor, Frank L. McSwain Sr. (Rest his soul) That was a great day.

Our first REAL argument was over something that I can't even remember. We ended up arguing for at least an hour over the smallest thing. I remember in the middle of the argument, he just abruptly got up and walked out. He had been gone for about ten minutes and I called my good friend Debra King at the time. She managed to calm me down and told me "he's just angry, he'll be back." During this time, the house was silent... completely. I wanted to kill him. Well, of course, Debra was right, and he eventually came back into the house in a huff still. I explained to him that after this, there would be NO WALKING OUT.... EVER. I'd never do that to him. I told him how walking out meant to me giving up to me, and I refused to be married to someone that wanted to give up so easily. He explained that he had been so frustrated, and he did not want to "be near me." Once we calmed down and decided to talk again, we came to an agreement that we would not argue for soooo long and that he would never walk out in the middle of a disagreement. He never did after that either. Boy, do I remember being angry.

I have no idea to this day what we fought about. But I know we would talk EVERYTHING to death. (Be careful what you pray for lol).

I remember our first vacation together. It was, in fact, our honeymoon and it was so much fun! We talked so much and had such a great time. We had received about $1,100.00 in gift monies, so we decided to drive to Florida for five days. We booked a hotel, made plans, and set off. On our drive down we laughed, talked, and discussed going higher in our lives and our marriage. We had such plans!

I remember us talking about getting better and taking our lives to a higher level. We actually passed a billboard that said something about stepping up to a higher level of performance AND THEN… we really got excited when this beautiful sports car passed us, and the plates read Higher Level. (Yes, Higher Level!) True story, as God is my judge. We shared experiences like that often in the beginning of our lives together. We knew we were destined to be together as they say.

On our honeymoon, Charles had his first rollercoaster ride with me. I still crack up at the fact that I shamed him into taking the ride with me as we were in the "Safari" as Busch Gardens, in Tampa. We loved Sea World, so we did that one day and Busch Gardens the other. We truly enjoyed Florida.

When we went to dinner one night at a place called Cooker, we met a great waitress who gave us our glasses because we were newlyweds. The glasses were very nice and had the word "Cooker" on them and are normally $15 a piece. It was funny because she smuggled them out to our car and left them by the back tires. I still can't believe she did that. She was a great waitress. I made sure we tipped her well.

One way we knew we were supposed to be together happened at our first family reunion as a married couple. Now, we have a great big awesome family, and we have a family reunion every year. Yes, every year. This year's reunion happened to be in Freeport, my home town. We were very excited because our relatives from St. Louis had been invited, and we had been in touch with our distant Hilton cousins. Two twins that actually lived in the St. Louis, Bellville, East St. Louis. Now my husband grew up in that area, and his father's family live in the Madison IL area. He had grown up playing as it turns out... right around the corner from my mother's first cousins, Annette and Jannette Hilton!

I was on one end of the room conversing with relatives and hadn't really been paying attention to much of where my hubby was at the time. Charles had actually stepped out of the room for a moment. Upon his return, he and my mothers' cousin Annette ran into each other and, several of my other relatives had been mingling and catching up.

I had not personally been introduced to our latest arrivals as I had several brothers and sisters I was catching up with and they were about to serve dinner. I had heard a bit of an "OMG" moment, and my Aunt Estelle and Aunt Sandra (Rest her soul) had actually been in conversation with Charles and our cousins. Well, they had just come to find out that not only did they know each other, but they had actually played together as kids! Talk about a wow moment! For all of us! It's kind of freaked me out, but it was also one of the neatest moments in our relationship. It reminded me of the term "Fate has intertwined us" Don't ask me where I'd heard that before, but it immediately came to mind when I remember that day. It was an awesome reunion that year, also a great first of many for us. I definitely remember family.

Our Wedding day. January 5, 1999 in our apartment. Off to a great beginning.

Our Wedding Ceremony at Mt. Pisgah Missionary Baptist Church 701 S. Lee, Bloomington IL.  BEST DAY EVER!

My favorite shots of Charles on our wedding day.  To quote him "Oh My Gosh what did I just do!"

Our reception on our June Wedding day.

# I Remember, His Art Work

The first time Charles shared his at work with me, I was excited and honored that he wanted to share something of his that was so personal with me. Now don't get me wrong; I was nervous because I felt I had a pretty critical eye for art. I had been exposed to some of the best art and artists while in college in art history. It was a very fun class for me, and I enjoyed art in general. I have to say how impressed I was. His work was simple but so elegant and interesting! He knew how to really capture facial expressions! I LOVED his "Smiling Lady"! She was beautiful. Her arms were spread wide as if she were getting ready to embrace a friend. She looked excited! He had drawn that free hand and not from a photo! Even when he doodled, it was amazing. We were heartbroken when we lost the piece in an apartment flood. I STILL can't stand that cheap ass landlord. Some other work I truly loved was just very simple doodles. He has one piece that was only two colors and just shape that he was "playing around with" Amazing! He would draw on napkins, grocery receipts, he would draw on anything that looked like it could be a blank canvas. And, I loved it.

My all-time favorite piece of art by Charles will forever be… "*The Finger Roll*"! The colors he chose reminded me of the Freeport High school Basketball team. This was a perfect image of a Dr. J in play right at the rim! It was so retro! This man's afro was huge, his fingers were over exaggerated, and I loved it! It was remarkable. In the picture, the shot was critical as you can see from his face but, he was enjoying every minute of it! I kept these pieces for August and Myles to see. They take after

Charles in this regard. Especially August. He is FOREVER doodling and drawing. EVEN in class. (Can you see my eyes rolling up in to my head at that one?) August is so much like Charles! He'd be very proud of him. He's so sensitive to others and so caring of what they think of him. He's growing up. Myles is also like him in the way he loves and describes images and stories. He's a wonderful storyteller. He has a wonderful vivid imagination. This image of Charles I completely remember cherishing. Especially since it's a trait that has been passed down to our boys. Daniel also shares the artistic gene. He has a great eye for photographs and graphics. I hope that he cultivates it when he goes on to college.

Now art is subjective, and all of his work and original pieces were so intriguing! Just his sketches around the house, on the white boards in the kitchen I had to capture! I loved his amazing talent. I have to admit his wonderful, natural talent made me jealous. I have NO talent for drawing. I can trace up a storm hahaha! However, I have only drawn a picture freehand a few times. It took a lot of time and more patience than I thought I had. I enjoyed my finished work. I enjoyed Charles's more. I remember I felt so special when he shared his *Star Troopers* comics with me. He loved that fact that I truly loved his work and his process. He had some stuff on a napkin, on a receipt, on basically any envelope or blank sheet of paper he could get his hands on. I loved finding stuff all of the time. He did a black and white mask once with just a simple red collar and won first prize at a contest in college. His "red and blue doodling shapes with was one of the most intricate things I saw him complete. It was just a simple piece, but it was beautiful. I could have NEVER had the patience for something like that, but it was just awesome! He got an honorable mention for that one as well. I wish I could find them to pass on to one of the boys. He was a fantastic artist. I remember loving his art. I remember.

This is some of his beautiful artwork.

Business logo and calling card.

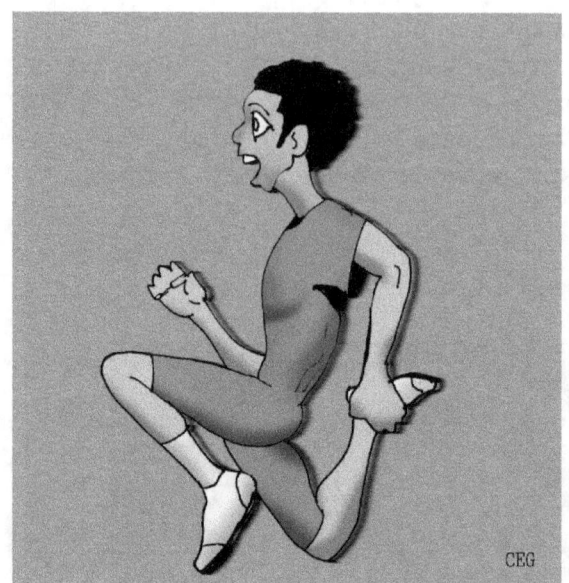
Scared Scott (I cracked up at this one)

His first draft of his graphic novel.

Star Curser

Art work connected to his story Charles continually worked to complete.

THE FINGER ROLL – My all-time favorite piece of Art by Charles Edward Griggs.   Art work was often seen on our refrigerator when he was "just doodling".    These doodles were all part of his wonderful imagination and storytelling ability.

This was on our refrigerator white board.

Beginning stages of some of his ideal art work.

These are just a few of the pictures that Charles worked on tirelessly in completing his graphic novel Titled Star Hoppers – His other novel the Adventures of Billy Phoenix what not just his favorite project but also a radio program he worked on with his nephew Antwon Griggs. Together their adventures were the stuff of "myth and legend!"

# I Remember, His Love for Music

I loved the way he was so passionate about it and about his favorite artists. Thelonious Monk and Myles Davis were amongst his key favorites. He often introduced me to a new artist and some next great Neo-Soul artist. I love Le Nubians, Soul to Soul and Van Hunt. My additional "Introduction to Music" via Charles Griggs was nothing short of interesting and full of new things! I loved the way he shared his love of Jazz. He had so many artists that were both old and new – I honestly could not keep up.

I remember sharing with Charles when I was growing up how the radio was my best friend. I could tell you who was singing the song and even who the back-up singers were if I really loved and artist. Huh, you better ask somebody. Most of the time, I got made fun of because I had listened to WLS out of Chicago growing up. I had no ideas about WGCI until I got to High School! Did I get talked about! Mostly because my favorite artist were Duran Duran, the Eurhythmics, Genesis, The Police, and The Beatles, all of whom I still love to this day! Yes, most all of them were British artist but again, I loved the radio. When I found out about WGCI, of course, I was late, but my flavor changed over time.

The one genre of music we both agreed that we did not like much at all was Gangsta-Rapp at the time, but we were good with Hip Hop and "Certain" Rapp Artists. Music was a staple part of our house. In addition to secular music that we both loved, I was and to this very day still, am a choir, singing Christian woman. So, I

LOVE gospel music. Don't get me wrong it was an interesting mix.

I will never forget one of our most humorous conversations was about music. He's made some off the wall comment about my tastes, and I got mad over it. He'd always say something until I listened to what he had on his iPod… he was listening to Nine Inch Nails, Pearl Jam and Blue Oyster Cult!! I could not believe it! He knew all of the words to the songs that he was playing too!! ALL OF THEM!! He even had the nerve to have some acid rock on his iPod! I was floored. We still laughed about his "Being caught with rock music on his iPod! I gave that man such a hard time over that one! I remember laughing.

Music kept us grounded and closely anchored with each other. It gave us the necessary solace we needed while we were going through the process of this life changing experience. Some of my favorite music and tunes I got at the suggestion of my husband Charles. I remember, we love music.

Two of my favorite photos of Charles at his favorite pastime, listening to music. His favorite artists, Thelonious Monk and Myles Davis was often heard around the house.

# I Remember, Daniel

As time progressed and Charles and I continued to get to know one another, he finally trusted me with what he felt was his greatest shame and secret. He had a son out of wedlock.

I had grown to know that Charles was a deeply proud and spiritual man but, felt a personal shame for having made a mistake with a girl that he was not married to. When we discussed this issue, I was quite frankly very troubled that he felt this way. No one is perfect

To be clear, he was NEVER ashamed of his child (my stepson Daniel). However, he was ashamed of himself for having given in to have sex with someone that he now (at that time) loathed as he put it.

She had lied and it ruined him. She was all things awful and manipulative in his eyes. He was hurt by the way she has treated him as a man; how she had humiliated him as Daniel was being born, and how she continued to squeeze and manipulate him by using Daniel as a tool to get money from him that he didn't have. (His words not mine) I know that at that time, Charles hated his ex. I tried many a day to convince him to stop being angry and to forgive; however, he was not inclined to do. So, it was my job to pray for both and to be the best stepmom for Daniel.

Charles' relationship with my stepson's mother was awful. I am a woman who never got in between the two. We had a respect issue once. And, I mean what I say when I say once. The day she called (we were still dating at the time), and she just had to reach Charles right now.

I stated to her, first of all, when you call my house looking for him, you say hello to me first, then you ask for him. If you can't do that, then you can't speak to him. She proceeded to get smart and started to tell me what she could do, and I hung up on her. She called back immediately of course, and before she could say anything else, and since I had warned her about her manners with me on the phone, and she again proceeded to tell me about what she needed, I hung up again. The next few rings, I let the answering machine pick up. I completely ignored the phone and did something to distract myself. Then about the fifth time she called me, she got a little "act right" and got the picture. She started with, "hello, may I please speak to Charles." I then answered politely yes, and gave the phone to Charles, who had been out at the time. I explained that we had rules and she would follow them. If not, she should not expect to speak to anyone in my home.

After this issue, she and I never argued, never once called each other out our names, or fought or anything like that. From the first time I met Daniel at 9 months old, Daniel was always a welcomed little love in our home. He had to be the most solid butterball; with the rounded face I had ever seen. He was too cute!!! I noticed right away that he was very observant. He never smiled until he really got used to seeing you and the first time, I met him in his pumpkin seat, he just stared at me. His eyes never wavered, he never smiled, but he followed me everywhere I went in the room. At first, it was unnerving having someone that little observing me and basically sizing me up. Hahaha… But that was fine. As he grew up, and once we got to know each other, Daniel and I were great together. I loved having him. He was a very interesting, artistic little man that loved to play. At least with me and we loved to have him. It would hurt my heart when we lived in Bloomington and ALL of us in his life (mom, Charles, grandma) were distracted or busy and had to "fit him in".

It killed Charles that we could not have full custody of him. Our biggest argument when it came to Daniel, was about him getting full custody of him. He wanted Daniel with us permanently and it was difficult for him to accept him being handled by her ex-boyfriend at *any* time. Let's just say we were all for getting him away from this man. I can truly say there was never any malice towards his ex when it came to this situation, it was her choice of a person that was around Daniel that we objected to. He treated Daniel poorly and, in our eyes, that is a cardinal unforgivable sin. You don't hurt our babies. EVER.

As Charles and I grew together, and as our relationship with Daniel's mother changed, eventually, things got much better. We had our difficult days as did his ex, but we all got through it and came to an understanding. Charles and she eventually got it together to a point. Daniel and I continued to build our relationship.

When I became pregnant with my first son August, Daniel and I really got to know each other. Once we decided on the baby's name, we shared it with Daniel. It was SUCH a fun conversation. We told him that the baby's name was going to be August. He says "August? Crinkling his nose, "Like the month?" I said "Yes, that's it." I then explained that his name comes from us thinking about the fact that we (Charles and I both) have an Augustus, and Augusta, Augustan or an Augustine on either side of our family. In addition to that, Charles's favorite play-write was August Wilson. So, we went with August.

Daniel laughed his cute charming little laugh and said "OK, but I think I'll call him October." We laughed and I tickled him until he relented. We could always talk and laugh. Each time I'd mention "baby August", in the future, Daniel would correct me and state "you mean baby October" with a grin. To this very day, I love that grin!
One of my favorite memories of Daniel, when he was a young one. By that, I mean, when he was between the age of four to about six and before August was born.

I remember once, we had been on our way to visit the family in Greenville as we were still living in Bloomington-Normal at the time. We had picked up Daniel from his grandmother's in Springfield. We were all in a great conversation laughing and joking and having a good time. As things and our conversation slowed down, Charles and I settled into listening to the radio and Daniel had his toys and was playing with things in the back seat.

All of the sudden, I hear him starting with this beat to a song I couldn't quite place... He starts singing "We're playing Bass kkk-ket -baaalll, we love that bass-kkketbaaall…" Over and over again with the beats in between. I am cracking up because that the only words he knew, and he was just hanging and enjoying himself. I tapped Charles who has been concentrating on the road and whispered for him to listen... He did and grinned from ear to ear, as Daniel continued to sing until he realized how quiet the car was because we had been listening to him sing.

Daniel looked up and started grinning at me because I was able to turn around to see him. Charles looked at him through the mirror and he was grinning too. Daniel stopped of course, and we both told him to not stop singing the song! Sing on!

Of course, he stopped but eventually when we stopped or pretended like we were not paying attention, he started up again. It was funny to hear him. He was so small but articulate. I loved the fact that he was such a smart boy!

That weekend we took family pictures and had a great time. Daniel got to visit with his cousins, and I was also getting to know them each a bit better. As Daniel grew, our times were both great and awful. His mother had her own issues, but we felt the brunt of them when Daniel was caught in the middle and we were left out. The worst times were when Charles had to go to court for anything concerning Daniel. He would get so frustrated with the prospect of even seeing Daniels mother that he'd often times not care to listen to the advice of the family.

My worse experience with this issue culminated one summer when she was with her ex-boyfriend (the one who replaced Charles in the delivery room) and they were determined to take Daniel. We knew that he treated Daniel poorly and were advised to seek custody of him. We ended up being ordered to give him back to her. They came to collect him on a Sunday afternoon in front of the courthouse in Greenville. ALL OF THE FAMILY was present, and the ex-boyfriend got lippy with my mother-in-law. (BIG MISTAKE on his part) I think things would have went smoothly had he kept his mouth shut. However, you know how stupid men can be when they get a little beside themselves? Well he decided stupid was the way to go that day.

This ex-boyfriend got WAAAAY besides himself. Got smart with my mother-in-law so much so, that my father-in-law (Rest his soul) had to be sure that the small pistol my mother-in-law "*MAY*" or may not have had or carried at one time, was put away so she couldn't find it. I don't ever recall seeing my mother-in-law (rest her beautiful soul) *that* angry, and she was never *that* angry…EXCEPT when it came to that man and his treatment of her grandson Daniel. Talk about wanting to spit nails??!! She did and we were all with her that day. I was hurt for Daniel and Charles both. My husband cried that day as Daniel left. Daniel was crying too. It was one of our toughest days.

Daniel was a true source of joy for Charles and me. Yes, Charles felt guilty for having him out of wedlock, but he loved him with all of his heart. He was so proud of him. Daniel and he could talk, and they had a great relationship. Some of the best times could be seen when they would hang out and in his photos. (See photos) We loved him being with us and I feel this was evident even if we were apart for long periods of time.

The boys, Daniel, August and Myles were his pride and joy. He'd be very proud of how they turned out today.

"The Boys" 2018

August's Kindergarten Graduation from St. Paul Academy.

Daddy and Myles. Just Hangin'

Daniel, All Smiles, All the time. (Age 8)

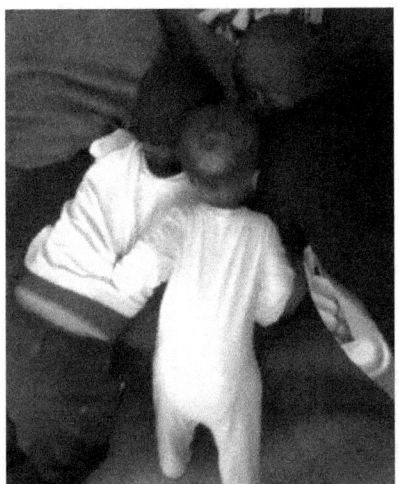
"The Boys" as I called them. They were all very interested in a Nintendo DS that one of the boys got for Christmas. I could not resist this shot. It was one of Charles's Favorites.

Summer, 2018. My sweet Daniel. I cannot believe he is so much taller than I am!

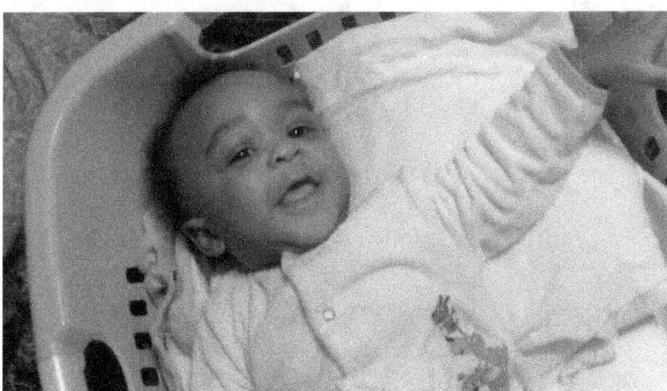

Charles was very proud of his family. The boys in particular gave him great joy. Some of his greatest times and our best memories were made with all of the boys.

August

Myles

## I remember, August and Myles

I remember the day I found out I was pregnant for the first time. For the past few weeks prior, I had gotten up as usual, gone to work, come home each day, *ate* my equivalent in the refrigerator, then went immediately to bed and often times, slept until the next day. I became aware of this on a Thursday. That next day, I took a pregnancy test to which I never got a clear result. Therefore, I took another one a week later to see a very clear result sign that was positive. I remember sitting on the side of the bathtub and calling to Charles. He was watching the TV and had not told him about the second test. So, I put on my big girl panties, and took a deep breath and called out… "Well, the rabbit died…" and waited for a response. I got a "What was that?" I laughed a repeated myself as I walked into the bedroom holding the pee stick as I called it. The look on his face was priceless. I had to ask him was he OK! SMH… Once he came back from being unconscious lol…he was excited and happy. See, we had talked about having kids but at the time we were married we did not want to begin a family. To be honest he did not want any kids because of the situation with his ex. He was very upset and insecure about being a father. He also did not want to be anything like his father. According to Charles, his father was an abusive alcoholic, and that left him with a very bad taste in his mouth and a sour opinion on fatherhood in general. I myself did not want to have children until we had been married a minimum of five years. My philosophy was this… I need to get to know you FOR REAL. If within that time I don't know you, then we do not need to have children together. I wanted to see how WE were together first. I did not like the idea of starting a family right away because I wanted to know my husband as just, he and I first. I know to this day *in my bones* that is was the right decision. You've heard that the first year of marriage is the hardest, right? Well it wasn't for us. It was years two and a half, three and four that were the worst of it. We went through a lot together. However, we did it together.

When I got pregnant, I was exactly five years that we had been married. So I guess my talk with the Lord was right on because on May 3, 2004, at 7:30 A.M. I gave birth to August Hilton Montgomery Griggs. My screaming bundle of joy was brought into this world with the assistance of his father. Which was comical because he was *no* help to me at all! He was fascinated with what was happening during the birth of his son and I didn't blame him at all. Truthfully, before the birth he was so obnoxious that I was glad he was a bit distracted. That was one the best days of my life. It made me so happy to have successfully given birth to a live baby boy who was healthy, had all ten of his fingers and toes! He was amazing! As he grew, I got to see firsthand just how amazing he was. As it turns out, Charles was a very amazing father as well. They had a great relationship right from the start.

Charles was very selfish when it came to August or Gus as we called him then. When we introduced him to the world of our families, Charles was the more protective of the two of us. At times, I had to remind him that I was his mother. Lol. It was comical but I could see the love in his face and in his actions. Never once did I have to ask him to change a diaper, feed him, or gather him when he was crying in the middle of the night. As August grew, they were the best of buddies. Charles was just as much a kid as August was and he made it very clear that he was enjoying every minute of being father to him. I remember him playing with him as an infant, as a toddler and as a young boy. They truly were the best of friends. I enjoyed watching every minute of it as well. I got to know Charles as a father and as a goofy friend to his sons. At the time both August, Daniel and Charles were inseparable. I loved it. As the boys grew, the many times that we had together helped to build us up and make us stronger. I remember a strong family unit.

The last addition to our family came when Charles and I were in transition as a family. August was five and a half, when we found out that I was pregnant again. My husband had been back in St. Louis earning his Master's degree in Counseling and we had moved up to Freeport about a year after we lost his mother. We were looking for new jobs all over the state. I had actually interviewed for several places literally, all over the country. My favorite being in Rhode Island New York. During the middle of that, Charles was accepted into the Master's program at UMSL. It was a year and a half, but he finished well! We were all very proud of him. I was especially proud, because I watched him go through so much to get it finished. At Thanksgiving that year, we were very close, and we missed each other. (Smiling) I remember having lots of fun that year with my husband. We were also very glad the he was finishing in the fall the following year. SO… at Christmas time when my sisters came home that year, I consequently wasn't feeling one hundred percent most of the time. I chalked it up to being "busy and stressed at work." Well, the joke was on me and my baby sister had called it correctly, I was in fact pregnant. When I called to tell Charles that a second rabbit had died, he laughed and stated that that was the best news he could have received that day. He'd had a rough week and he needed some good news. That night, during our nightly conversation I sprung it on him that he was going to be a daddy for a third time. He was excited because he wanted a girl. I did not think that he had actually would have ever wanted another child, so I was extremely nervous when I told him. In my opinion, he took the news rather well.

We laughed about it later because he said when he hung up after our call, he kind of freaked out. However, at the same time he was excited because that very same night he called all of his sisters to share the news. On August 20, 2010, at 10:21 a.m., I successfully gave birth to a very lively Myles Emory Griggs. This Seven-pound seven-ounce boy was the second greatest thing I had ever seen. My first was my son August. Myles was every bit as health and cute as August had been. All ten fingers and toes were in place. Myles was a particular favorite with Charles. Not that he was choosing one son over another, he just liked the fact the Myles was a bit more animated and into conversation as a baby than August may have been. I remember how much Charles loved his children. From the very beginning, he was all in. He loved spending any time with the boys and especially loved playing with them. Some of my favorite memories are of Myles, his father and myself and the pictures I took of them all playing together. As Myles, August and Daniel all grew it was Charles who kept them all at attention with his creative antics, humor and activity. Myles was only two years old when we lost Charles, but e very clearly remembers the love he felt with Charles. All my boys to this day remember how much fun their father was. I remember a lot of love and fun with our children. I remember love.

## I Remember, The Illness That Killed Him

My husband was diagnosed with an illness called Polymyositis. It is a chronic inflammation of all the major muscles. Meaning the Heart, Lungs, Spleen, Pancreas, Liver, and Intestines - all of them. It fills up all of your major organs with fluid and makes them work twice as hard to stay working. It is awful and is often misdiagnosed. After this diagnosis, Charles was ill and was gone within a year and a half.

During that time, Charles had become very angry at his life, the sickness taking over his health and the fact that Daniel was becoming a defiant teenager.

At the beginning of his illness, Charles and Daniel had a tremendously hard time getting along. Their relationship was strained a great deal of the time we were together. It was an extremely difficult time.

Charles had come home, with oxygen from the hospital after a two-week stay with a diagnosis of pneumonia. It was a Thursday. Therefore, everything after that was high alert.

I had been out of the house, getting Charles his medications and doing what the Dr. told us he needed. We were not home long when we got a knock at the front door. It was the nurse practitioner form the VA hospital. We had followed up from his hospital visit. She had come with the results of his tests. She told us that we immediately had to get Charles to the hospital in either Rockford or Madison. His lab results and EKG were off the charts and she felt he needed to be hospitalized immediately. Today was one of the most emotional days that I will ever remember.

It is at this point that my life took a seriously hard turn to the far left. We decided that we could get to Rockford Memorial faster than we could the VA hospital in Madison, as it was an hour and a half away. My family (mom and dad, bless them both) took the boys. My sister Estelle and I drove Charles to Rockford Memorial Hospital where he was immediately admitted to the ER. He was there about 35 minutes and the Doctor came in to tell us he needed to be admitted immediately. While he was in the ER, the readings and tests indicated that he had a silent heart attack. Charles broke down. He was angry and did *not* want to be admitted to the hospital. He had just gotten out. He was taken right away to the ICU where he stayed for the next 4 weeks. It was the roughest time of my life. Prior to his begin admitted to the hospital. Charles had been in the hospital in Freeport approximately two weeks. 14 very long days. He had been tested, poked and prodded so much that I complained to the management of the department regarding the lack of progress. They never came up with any answers.

During this next 4 to 6-week period. I had to continue to work. Charles remained in the ICU at Rockford Memorial. I was back and forth to the doctor's office & hospital every day over my lunch hour as I worked in Rockford College (University) at the time. Every day after work, I went to visit my husband unless they were running tests. I kept him informed and I kept him company. When he was released into Rehab, I was there.

He was at Van Matre, in Rockford, which was just around the corner from *then* Rockford College (University).

Over the next year, my husband progressively went into organ failure. This took on the form of weakening bones, two bowel surgeries, constant nausea and vomiting; a four-week stay in intensive care before a clear diagnosis was given; two weeks in rehabilitation and then more rehabilitation at home. I remember caring for Charles in the early hours. It was so hard to watch my big strong man turn into such a frail struggling man. He hated this sickness. He didn't understand this sickness. I hated this sickness and I didn't understand this sickness. He didn't like to toll it was taking on him. I hated watching the toll it took on him. As he grew ill in the beginning, Charles could not go to work. He hated not being able to work. He was NEVER one to sit around and do nothing. Even when Charles was unemployed, he *was not* "just doing nothing" about it. He was actively seeking a job both online and in person. If not, he was working around the house. He ABSOLUTELY REFUSED to leave the house before 3:00 p.m. when he was unemployed because he didn't want to look like a "shiftless thug" as he put it.

He was a very proud man. When he was not able to provide for us by working regularly and had to rely on me (and my family and I on GOD), he felt broken about that. I would of course, remind him of the vows we took and said to each other before God... *For better or for worse, for richer or for poorer, in sickness and in health.*

I had to help him to remember that I took those vows with him, and I took them very seriously. He knew this, and we would talk until he would sleep. I remember when my husband was sick how he would cry because he couldn't quite understand why this was happening to him. He was uncomfortable physically most all of the time. He was also nauseated, hungry but could only eat or take in liquids but vomited that up a lot too. I sometimes remember the only comfort he was afforded many nights was my rubbing his head holding his hands and crying with him. He was sick and throwing up so often that it scared us both. I remember telling mom that he was wasting away because he couldn't keep anything down. He was barely eating anymore, and he was drinking only water or a few sips of Gatorade. It was horrific. He did not have cancer, but the treatments for his disease were just like cancer treatments.

The first time we drove to Madison for his appointment, it was an all-day appointment. He had to sit with a slow drip of whatever the steroid medication was for exactly eight hours. It was a LOOOOONG time for me, but we talked, and he rested most of the time. It was so tough to be there as a healthy person and seeing several people having similar treatments. I stayed when Charles wanted me there. We would hold hands, while he slept, I would read a magazine and sometimes snooze too. I would read to him from books and magazines as well. He loved that. I mostly just let him rest. The next visit was for exactly six hours, then five hours and the last one was four hours.

The time we spent at the hospital during his treatment was some of the hardest time for us together. Charles was never confident in any of the treatments, but he was willing to do them because we wanted his health back.

We wanted his life back. We never pictured this part. In sickness and in health is no joke. He and I talked about God's plan very little during this time. It was excessively hard for him. He had lost faith a bit. He didn't want to hear much about that when I'd pray or even how often I talked to the Lord on his behalf. He was, of course, a very spiritual man, and knew, "What it felt like to be in the presence of the Holy Spirit." I would tell him yeah, that's great however, we still had to talk to God.

The Song "Just a little Talk with Jesus" often comes to mind. I will never understand how such a spiritual person could be so negative. However, up to this point, I never understood what this time in our lives was doing to our collective lives either. Up to that point in my life, I only knew how to lean on the Lord and have faith in His promises. Even though such a horrific experience, I HAD to lean on God. Yes. My family was back up, but it was and continued always to be, God first.

Even through our worst arguments, we would always put God first. We loved The Lord and truly relied on Him throughout our relationship. It was tough to continue to remain faith-filled when Charles was at his worse. His sickness manifested itself in every area of our lives.

I remember when I notice how things we actually taking their toll on me as well. I remember clearly getting up one morning. It was cold and I remember taking Myles to my mothers. I honestly do not remember anything after that except I am sitting in the parking lot on my job looking down at the keys in my hands. My boss Brad Knotts knocking on my window and asking me if I was ok. I think the look I had worried him because he stayed outside my car and walked with me into the building. He took me into his office, and I told him what we had been going through. To this day, I still cannot remember driving myself to work. Thank God, for praying parents because I must have truly been using *The Force* that day. I was very grateful for Brad, his counsel and comfort.

## My Family Remembers

My mother says she remembers the first time she met Charles. It was also at the time of or TRUE "First Date." Charles had asked me out, and I told him that he needed to meet me at church, and we would go from there. The weekend he decided to show up, my parents were in town! I said to myself that if he wanted to be with me at all, it would be 100% on my terms.

One of my conditions was that he meet me at church, and we would go from there. Well, he showed up. I was of course in the choir stand when he got there so I actually would not get to speak to him until after service. When I finished – about 10 minutes after service, there he stood in the vestibule with his hands folded TALKING TO MY MOTHER! (Can you see my eyes rolling heavenward SMH)?

I thought to have introduced them. However, my mother being the world friendliest social butterfly had already spoken to about 90 people (no real exaggeration intended ha ha ha..), so just as I made my way to the front of the church, mom had finished talking to Charles and had started off to find my dad. Our conversation was a bit awkward. However, we got through it. My mother's impression was spot on and to quote her, "the man wants to marry my daughter." She confessed to me later. Now do not get me wrong, I know some people have a gift of predictions however, THIS prediction, at THIS particular time, was not funny. I honestly did not intend to see this man at all, whether he showed up or not. I was impressed he actually had shown up AND met my parents on the same day. That said something. In all honesty, I truly did not intend to date him at all. God had other plans.

According to my Aunt Estelle, she remembers whenever we visited my parents, and my family was home, Charles would take a knee right behind my moms' couch and telling the best stories! He would be talking about all his travels in the Navy and how he learned so many great things. One of my favorite gifts from him was a genuine China Tea Set from him then he'd acquired when he was in Japan. My mother still has the cups from that set. My aunt remembers that he was sometimes reclusive and at times, it was hard to really get close to him. However, she also recalled that he was a wonderful storyteller and that he had a great sense of humor.

Charles in his element. Charles enjoyed being in the Navy. He was very proud of the work he did there. He was honorably discharged after his four-year term.

# *I Remember –*
## *As told by my Children*

When I asked my children what they remember best about their father, I got some thoughtful answers and at first, some long faces. I had hoped this process would not be painful for them. However, as it turns out, I have some very cool kids. They have wonderful memories of their father.

It was amazing to me how much of Charles my sons remembered.

## *August Remembers –*

August remembers playing with Charles and having a wonderful time, especially with his puppet shows and action figures. He loves Star Wars and Star Trek because of his father. He loves comic books and the characters because he and Charles would draw stuff like that together.

One of my favorite photos has August playing in a box that Charles eventually turned into a puppet theatre that he stayed in all the time! August remembers playing with his father and making films with his brother Daniel. They had some great times.

You can check them out at the following YouTube web addresses.

https://www.youtube.com/watch?v=YTZLESNZ008&t=298s
(August and Daniel)
https://www.youtube.com/watch?v=2XzpZ9GH0Zw
(Myles and Daniel)

https://www.youtube.com/watch?v=UyJGu79RWgA
(August and Daniel at Patriots Park)

https://www.youtube.com/watch?v=rOXqULlTi7s
(August Dancing with Bow Legged Lou)

## *Myles Remembers-*

Myles had great memories of playing with daddy and talking about "stuff" as he put it. He remembers sitting with him and talking to him about the puppets and Dr. Coz. We cried quite some time together when we would look at photos of Charles and Myles together. When Myles asks me, (which is quite often) we like to sit together, and I share stories with him about Charles. His favorite memory of his father is when they made a short video with his daddy that was with just the two of them. We loved watching this one over and over again. Myles likes to remember how much fun his father was with both he and August.

I would love to send you a link however, this one is still attached to Charles phone. This is the one piece of him I still have that actually belonged to him. He didn't really have much he cared about in the end. I thought to give it to one of the boys, eventually I will. However, my children have asked me to keep it. At least until I can get the video and pictures. Myles remembers how his father would tell great stories. He loved sitting on his lap and listening to his voice and falling asleep.

## *Daniel Remembers*

When I asked Daniel to give me some insight as to what he remembered of his father, it took him a few minutes to respond. I know that he loved him, but I also wanted him to put some real thought into his answer.

He remembers growing up, knowing that he was loved. He remembers how he loved being around his father and how they were so creative together. He loved playing with his action figures with him and that he had so much fun with the puppet shows. He particularly remembers the videos with dad and August as well.

He remembers how often when he had to leave, and that it made him sad. But he also knew that he would see him again soon. He remembered he felt unsure of himself and of me at times. When we talked at the hospital in Bellville at the time of Charles's passing, Daniel said that he thought I was angry with him because he fought with him while he was sick. I explained that at the time, I was mad at *both* of them. At the time his father needed his support not his anger or misunderstanding. I explained the whole situation with Charles was hard on all of us. But we always loved him, we missed him when he was not with us and cared for him always. Daniel was also assured that Charles loved him with all his heart. That he was extremely proud of him and wanted only the best for him. It made Charles sick and sad when he was not in communication with him regularly. Charles often agonized over the lack of communication. He never wanted to have that kind of relationship with his eldest son. He wanted me to let Daniel know that he loved him no matter what. We talked for about an hour and cleared the air regarding a lot of misunderstanding that were dictated by Charles and his resentment towards Daniels mother.

Daniel knows to this day that Charles and I love him tremendously no matter what. It was a very healthy relationship for him because I have known Daniel since he was nine months old.

He spent a great deal of time traveling between mom, grandma, and us. It wasn't easy for us for that matter. However, I know through it all he felt the love and the sense of family from us all.

He remembers that his father seemed angry a lot, but when we talked, we spoke about how Charles never explained to him that he was mad at himself most of the time. I wanted him to know clearly that he was loved and that we still love him no matter what.

Daniel wanted to be sure of his father's love, and we assured him of this together on his death bed. When it was all said and done Daniel knew without question, he was loved by his father and that his being part of our lives was a welcome and would never change. Now don't get me wrong I am no Jada Pinkett-Smith. It took more than a minute for me to even speak to Daniel's mother civilly. That was due to the mood Charles set with us regarding her. Now we are mature adults, and I feel mutual respect is there, that was not able to be cultivated before some growth and prayer for and from the both of us.

I'm happy to say that we have a friendly and communicative relationship today.

## Picking Up the Pieces

There is no such thing as a perfect relationship. I had to come to grips with the fact that marriage, ALL MARRIAGE, takes work. I worked my ass off within my marriage. I loved my husband. I meant what I said when I said in sickness and in health. We may have had our differences, but our love and our marriage were real. Our love and friendship were always there. I was his faithful wife to the very end of his days. I remember when Charles was visiting his sisters during the last few months of his illness how I put several thousand miles on my car traveling back and forth between St. Louis, Bellville, and University of Wisconsin Hospital and Freeport holding things together.

I want to acknowledge to everyone that my marriage was not perfect. Charles and I had good days, bad days, arguments, disagreements, and days we did not speak. Nevertheless, through it all, we loved each other. We chose to be a husband and wife. We decided to keep other people out of our relationship and to tough it out in all aspects. YES, through sickness and health was serious to us both. In the end, I honored my husband.

I went through it. He passed away, and I lived through it.

However, I had a lot to learn and a lot to live for. I learned FIRST, after everything, I had to let go of my anger toward him. I had to let go of being angry that in the last years of his life, Charles was just not happy, and there was nothing I could do about it.

I had to let go of being angry that he did not tell me until after we had been married for seven years, that he was diagnosed in the Navy with clinical depression.

Then I was angry because I had turned myself inside out to please him because of not having this knowledge!

Then I was just angry that he is gone! My best friend is gone, and I can't tell him about all the crap that I go through daily!

I had to let go of being angry, that angry because he left my children and me at the prompting of a family relation who did not care to acknowledge they knew nothing about our marriage or us.

I had to let go of being angry that his associated "family" had a whole lot to say but NEVER ONCE during the time of ANY of my husband's numerous hospital stays, surgeries, or sicknesses, not once to this day have they asked about my young children or even if they needed anything. I had to let go of being angry that I had to pick up the pieces alone after his death.

I had to let go of being angry that I was painted as the problem he had in his life. That I was the cause of his death! Bullshit! Oh Yes, was I angry about that!

Now, I can't say anything to him about all of the stuff we were looking forward to doing. I had to do alone or with someone else!

I can't tell him how awesome all three of our boys are!

I can't show him the hard work we did paid off!

I can't share with him all of the great plans for our boys we wanted and just how smart and artistic they are.

I can't just sit and talk to him and listen to music with him.

I can't just vent to him when I am truly pissed off to the highest point of pissetivity (as we put it). I can't do any of that!

I had to let go of being angry that he is not here to discipline our boys or to guide them as only he could have done.

I had to let go of being angry, I mean truly angry that he's not here to advise me when to be quiet or sit still or to let him handle, it anymore!

I had to let go of being angry plain just angry! UGGGH!!

However, through all of this anger, I was grateful.

I am still grateful for the love we found together and the life we created together.

I am grateful for the friends that we made, that we have still and, that are with us now that he is gone.
I am grateful that my mother, father, and my family taught me how to rebuild and to do all the God has called me to do as a wife, sister-in-law, and friend.

I am grateful, that I chose to listen to God when he gave me answers to my prayers.

I am grateful for the three children that God gave me with Charles.

I am grateful that I am STILL working on my anger through love.

The gratitude and love that the Lord God and my family gives to me, I hope to return to my children and them to others.

I am grateful that I was raised to forgive.

I am grateful that someone somewhere prayed for me.

I am grateful that strength comes from the Lord and not from others.

I am grateful for so many things.

I live each day with a grateful heart. It is not at all easy!!

SO many times, and I wanted to just cuss somebody out when I'd get angry at stupid advice given to my husband and or to me. I will never be able to put in to words how grateful I am that my mother taught me to pray and to be grateful to the Lord for it all. No matter how hard it has been.

I am grateful for the journey I was on with Charles.

Because of his suffering, I am also grateful that that journey was over.

I remember being grateful; he was no longer in pain and that he could let go of all of his worries.

How do you tell someone goodbye, that you planned to spend the rest of your life with? What do you do when that time is cut short?

You are in the middle of your life, and he, your love, your friend becomes deathly ill?

How do you move on when you don't know why God chose to take him from you?

How do you forgive yourself?

How do you forgive the wrongs you felt were directed directly at you by your in-laws?

How do you forgive them?

How do you let go of the past and embrace a bright future?

You believe. You trust God. You Pray - A LOT!!

You lean on your praying family.

You become stronger, and you THANK GOD for all that you have.

That is what I did. I was the only thing I could do.

Moving forward, I found a great poem recently on Facebook of all places that truly sums up how I feel. I'm not sure of the author, but I acknowledge you whoever you are, and I am grateful for your words.

*For My Husband in Heaven...*
*They Say there's a reason*
*They say time will heal*
*Neither time nor reason*
*Will Change how I feel*
*Gone are the days*
*We used to share but, in my heart,*
*You are always there*
*The gates of memories will never close*
*I miss you more than anybody knows*
*We love and miss you every day.*
*Till we meet again*
*Always and forever love you*

*...Author Unknown*

We lost Charles to what the Doctors called Poly-myositis. This chronic inflammation of all of the major muscles causes his heart and other organs to over inflate and then have to work too hard to sustain him. Natural causes is on the death certificate but ultimately his organs failed. We will forever miss him.

I waited until the boys asked me to visit their father's grave. It took 3 years. I would make the visit each year by myself and the boys wanted to go together. It was beautiful and the hardest thing I have ever had to get through aside from laying him to rest. We got though it and we only cried half way home. When I would be alone. I cried the whole way home. Having them with me this time made it easier, as we talked and shared loving and funny memories of family friends and Charles.

My boys placing flowers at their father's grave.

The Gravesite, Jefferson Barracks, MO.

The one day his family came to visit when Charles was in the hospital in intensive care. It was a great day for all of us.

Our first family portrait after Myles was born. Charles hated this picture. The background was dark, and he said we all looked greasy. I agreed but I loved the fact that we were together.

It's time to let go. It's time to begin to truly heal. It's time for our lives to take on a new direction.

I'm looking forward to the future and new life, new love and new adventure.

Thank you, Charles.

I will love you always,

Michelle

# ABOUT THE AUTHOR

Photo taken by August Griggs (9 yr. old)

Michelle D. Griggs M.S, M.S

Michelle received her first Master's degree from Illinois State University in the area of Curriculum and Instructions with a Diversity focus. Her second Masters is in Special Education with a K-12 cross-categorical focus. She has worked in Higher Education for Rockford University (RC) as the Director of the Kobe-Regents Center for Global Education and with Greenville University (GC) as the Director of Multicultural Education. She is currently employed with the Freeport School District as the SELF (Social Emotional Learning Facilitator) classroom teacher.

Michelle currently lives in Freeport, IL. Where she is an active mother of two strong boys, August and Myles. She works with the Boys & Girls Club in the after-school program and as a summer camp counselor. Michelle is also the Sunday School Superintendent with the St. Paul Missionary Baptist Church of Freeport, IL. She sings in the choir and is a Choir Directress.

In her spare time, Michelle enjoys reading, writing, travel spending time with her children and family.

She may be contacted at: MichelleDGriggs3@gmail.com

www.ingramcontent.com/pod-product-compliance
Lightning Source LLC
LaVergne TN
LVHW051510070426
835507LV00022B/3030